THE LOST KING: AKHENATON

KRISTI MC CRACKEN

Artesian Press
P.O. Box 355, Buena Park, CA 90621
www.artesianpress.com

Nonfiction
Ancient Egyptian Mystery Series

The Lost King: Akhenaton	1-58659-205-X
Audio Cassette	**1-58659-121-5**
Audio CD	**1-58659-355-2**
The Lords of Kush	1-58659-207-6
Audio Cassette	1-58659-123-1
Audio CD	1-58659-357-9
Mummies	1-58659-208-4
Audio Cassette	1-58659-124-X
Audio CD	1-58659-358-7
The Great Pyramid	1-58659-206-8
Audio Cassette	1-58659-122-3
Audio CD	1-58659-356-0
The Rosetta Stone	1-58659-209-2
Audio Cassette	1-58659-125-8
Audio CD	1-58659-359-5

Cover photo courtesy of National Museum of Scotland
Project Editor: Molly Mraz
Graphic Design: Tony Amaro
©2004 Artesian Press

 *Artesian Press*   ISBN 1-58659-205-X

CONTENTS

Word List

adobe (uh-DOE-bee) A sun-dried brick material used for building.

Akhenaton (ahk-NAHT-n) The "rebel Pharaoh" who changed Egyptian religion and worshipped only one god.

Amarna (uh-MAHR-nuh) Akhenaton's beautiful desert city.

Amenhotep III (ah-muhn-HOE-tep) The father of Akhenaton, and the richest Pharaoh of ancient Egypt.

Amun-Ra (AH-muhn-rah) King of the Egyptian gods, the joining of the Theban god Amun and the sun god Ra.

ankh (angk) A cross that was the symbol of life.

Ankhes (AHNK-ehs) A queen of Egypt, first married to King Tut, then to Aye.

archeologist (ark-ee-AHL-uh-jist) A scientist who tries to find the truth about things that happened in the past.

Aton (AHT-n) Akhenaton's god, the sun disk. Aton represented the spirit and shape, or disk, of the sun.

Aye (rhymes with *pie*) A high priest who ruled with King Tut and was Pharaoh after Tut died.

cuneiform (kyoo-NEE-uh-form) Having a wedge shape.

hieroglyphs (HIE-ruh-gliffs) Pictures that stood for words or sounds in the ancient Egyptian religious writing.

Horemheb (HOR-em-heb) A general of the Egyptian army. He became Pharaoh after Aye died.

Horus (HOHR-ehs) An Egyptian god who was the protector of the Pharaoh.

Kiya (KEE-yah) Akhenaton's later wife.

Nefertiti (nef-uhr-TEE-tee) Akhenaton's royal wife, who was very beautiful.

papyrus (puh-PIE-russ) A plant used to make a kind of writing paper and whose reeds could be woven to make rope.

Ra (rah) The sun god and most important god to many ancient Egyptians.

sarcophagus (sar-COFF-uh-gus) A king's stone coffin.

scarabs (SCAR-uhbs) Beetle-shaped plaques.

Smenkhkare (smeng-KAR-eh) One of Egypt's Pharaohs who was thought to be a brother of King Tut.

Thebes (theebz) The city in ancient Egypt where most of the Pharaohs lived and built temples to their many gods.

Tiy (tee) Amenhotep III's wife and a very powerful queen. Tiy helped her son Akhenaton become Pharaoh.

Tutankhamen (too-tahng-KAH-muhn) Also called "King Tut," he became Pharaoh when he was only eight years old.

Chapter 1

Egypt is an ancient country filled with thousands of years of history. It is the home of the Sphinx, the pyramids, and the Valley of the Kings. It is a land filled with unsolved mysteries. Perhaps the greatest mystery surrounds a Pharaoh who ruled more than three thousand years ago. His name was Akhenaton (ahk-NAHT-n).

For many years, archeologists (ark-ee-AHL-uh-jists) and Egyptologists (people who study ancient Egypt) have been puzzled by this Pharaoh. Many strange things happened when Akhenaton ruled.

Some 200 miles south of the city of Giza lies the once-lost city built by

Akhenaton. It is buried beneath the desert sands. Many Pharaohs before Akhenaton lived in a city called Thebes (theebz). Why did Akhenaton leave Thebes and build this city in the desert?

Ancient Egyptians believed in many gods and had temples for them. In Akhenaton's city, only one god was worshipped--the sun disk, Aton (AHT-n). Some people thought Akhenaton was a "religious rebel" and a traitor because he did not follow the old ways. Why did he make up a new religion?

The artwork from Akhenaton's rule is different from earlier artwork. For thousands of years before Akhenaton, Pharaohs always looked handsome and strong in drawings, like warriors ready for battle. The drawings and statues of Akhenaton show a man with a long head and face and a strange body. Why did Akhenaton let his artists show him as he really looked?

Akhenaton's city was destroyed

when he died. With wide streets and pools of water, the city was an island of beauty in the middle of a desert. Why would anyone destroy a city full of beautiful palaces and temples?

Egyptologists have tried for many years to put together the few facts they have about Akhenaton's life, but it is a difficult task. Akhenaton's name was taken off the list of Pharaohs. He was erased from all official records of the time. His temple to Aton was destroyed and his tomb was taken apart stone by stone. Who tried to change history, and why?

©National Museum of Scotland

This stone picture of Akhenaton shows his long head and face. Akhenaton was the first Pharaoh to let his artists show how he really looked.

Chapter 2

Akhenaton's father, Amenhotep III (ah-muhn-HOE-tep), was Pharaoh during one of the greatest periods of Egyptian history. This period is called "The Golden Age of Egypt." Egypt was so powerful during Amenhotep III's rule that no other country dared to anger him. They were afraid to start a war with Egypt.

All the Pharaohs before Akhenaton were famous for their bravery in battle. To prove his courage and strength as a ruler, Amenhotep III killed more than a hundred lions in the first ten years of his rule. However, Akhenaton was not athletic like his father. He could not become a great hunter, so he needed to find another way to become famous.

Some Egyptologists think that Amenhotep III was the richest Pharaoh of ancient Egypt. Princes from foreign countries came to him to learn about Egypt. Afterward, the princes went back to their own countries to rule. They sent Amenhotep III gifts and gold, which made him even richer.

With his riches, Amenhotep III built many beautiful temples to his gods to make them happy. He thought that if the gods were happy, Egypt would be rich and powerful. Amenhotep III built a temple at Luxor, near the city of Thebes. He also completed the Temple of Amun (AH-muhn), which honored the sun god Ra (rah). Amenhotep III also built a temple showing himself as a king and a god.

Amenhotep III had a large harem, or group of wives. Many of his wives were princesses from the lands around Egypt. This made him even more wealthy. One princess from Asia brought him more than three hundred servants!

This statue of the god Amun comes from the Temple of Amun at Karnak, built by Amenhotep III.

Amenhotep III did not pick a princess from his royal family to be his queen, as Pharaohs usually did. Instead, he chose a woman from another country who was not of royal blood. Her name was Tiy (tee). Later, Akhenaton would do the same thing.

Queen Tiy was a powerful woman, and Amenhotep III loved her very much. Before they married, he had artisans create beetle-shaped plaques, called scarabs (SCAR-uhbs), to announce his marriage. To make his wife happy, he later had a huge lake and a pleasure boat built for her.

Akhenaton, whose real name was Amenhotep IV, was the youngest child of Amenhotep III and Queen Tiy. He had four sisters and one brother. The sisters were all princesses, and his brother was called a high priest. When Akhenaton was a child, it seems there were no titles or honors given to him.

Akhenaton's picture did not appear with his family in the many drawings that decorated the temple walls. There was no statue of him with the statues of the royal family. Did the royal family ignore the youngest son? Were they ashamed of their strange-looking child, with his wide hips and long head, fingers, and toes?

After Amenhotep III ruled for thirty years, he had a big party called a Sed-festival. He told the priests to research thousands of years of old records until they found a proper ceremony. They found a ceremony that they believed would change the Pharaoh into the sun god, Ra. With the help of many priests and high court officials, Amenhotep III performed this magical ceremony.

Amenhotep III may have used an illusion or magic trick to make the Egyptians believe that he really had become the sun god, Ra. The people had always seen the Pharaoh as the god Horus (HOHR-ehs), the protector of the Pharaoh. This was not enough for Amenhotep III. He wanted to be worshipped as the sun god!

Amenhotep III became known as "The Sun King." He wore three strands of large gold beads around his neck like a collar. Before him, only dead Pharaohs wore this type of collar. It meant they were joined with the sun god, Ra. Many historians believe that Amenhotep III wore the gold collar to show that he was the living sun god. When Akhenaton became Pharaoh, he, too, wore a gold collar to show he was a living god.

Amenhotep III ruled Egypt for more than thirty years. He was a successful hunter, politician, and builder. When Amenhotep III died, Egyptians believed that he had gone to the glorious afterlife. The next Pharaoh would become the new Horus, the hawk-headed god. At the time of Amenhotep III's death, it was written, "The hawk has flown to heaven and another stands in his place."

This other "hawk" was his eighteen-year-old son, Akhenaton. Egyptologists believe that Queen Tiy used her power and influence with Amenhotep III to make her ugly son Pharaoh.

How would this strange young Pharaoh change Egypt? Would his own actions lead to his downfall?

Chapter 3

In 1352 B.C., Akhenaton became Pharaoh of Egypt after his father's death. Like Pharaohs before him, he began his rule in the city of Thebes. His first official act as Pharaoh was to build a temple at Karnak. Karnak was a special area of temples in Thebes. There were many temples for the different gods that the Egyptians worshipped, especially the sun god, Ra. Akhenaton's temple showed for the first time how different he was from other Pharaohs.

All the Pharaohs of Egypt had worshipped many gods and built temples to them. Akhenaton built his temple in honor of only one god, the sun disk, Aton. No Pharaoh had ever done that before.

The structure of Akhenaton's temple was also different from other temples because it had no roof. He wanted his temple open to the light of Aton.

The artwork on Akhenaton's temple walls was unlike any that had come before it. In the old temples, the walls were covered with pictures of many Egyptian gods that were part animal and part human. The drawings on the walls of Akhenaton's temple show the sun disk with life-giving rays and long hands holding ankhs (angks), the symbol of life. The sun disk's fingers are long and thin, like Akhenaton's.

Also on the temple walls are pictures of Akhenaton and his wife. The pictures show the happy husband and wife enjoying each other's

This ankh is from Amarna, the city Akhenaton built.

©Photograph courtesy of the Rosicrucian Museum, San Jose, CA

company and praying to Aton. Like his father, Akhenaton did not marry a woman with royal blood. His wife was named Nefertiti (nef-uhr-TEE-tee). People still talk about her great beauty even today.

The pictures on the temple walls also show other surprising things. In several of the pictures, Nefertiti is alone or with her daughters. Usually, women were not included in Egyptian art. If they were, they were shown smaller in size than the Pharaoh.

Inside the temple gate is a picture of Nefertiti and one of her daughters. On many of the pillars, the mother and daughters are shown giving offerings to Aton. In one drawing, a daughter is playing with an Egyptian rattle. Many of the drawings are just of Nefertiti and her daughters, without Akhenaton. This meant that Nefertiti was probably more important than other wives, and she was Akhenaton's equal.

For the Egyptian people, the strangest and most frightening thing about Akhenaton's temple was the fact that only one god was pictured on the walls. For two thousand years, the Egyptians had worshipped many gods. They believed that the different gods made the country successful and would help them in the afterlife.

Akhenaton's temple showed the people of Thebes that their Pharaoh believed in only one god. For the first time in recorded history, a Pharaoh had turned away from the known religion and started one of his own. Historians believe that many Egyptians--especially the priests and the craftsmen who made things for the gods--were angry and afraid of losing their way of life.

Most Egyptians probably wanted things to stay the same. Perhaps they worried about how they would get to the afterlife without their many gods.

Egyptologists think that Akhenaton

felt that his power was getting weaker after the Egyptians found out what he believed. Sometime in the first few years of his rule, Akhenaton held a Sed-festival, as his father did. This festival was meant to give the Pharaoh more strength in case his power got weak. However, it was not usually held until the thirtieth year of a Pharaoh's rule.

Proof of Akhenaton's fear for his own safety and that of his family is seen in tomb drawings. Some of the drawings show him leaving the palace with armed troops. Other pictures show guards running behind his horse-pulled cart, called a chariot. Other drawings show guards bowing low, with their spears to the ground, as he enters the temple. Several pictures show guards with sticks protecting the queen and princesses.

Unlike his father, Akhenaton seems to have been a peace-loving ruler. No record or drawing has been found that shows Akhenaton leading troops into battle the way other Pharaohs did. His feelings about peace are shown in a song of praise to Aton.

By rejecting the old gods and worshipping a single god, Akhenaton made powerful enemies in Thebes. People were frightened of the change. The priests were angry and afraid that they would lose their titles and jobs. Akhenaton must have heard the people complain, because he hinted that bad things were said about him.

In his fifth year as Pharaoh, Akhenaton decided to leave Thebes. He changed his name from Amenhotep IV to Akhenaton. Then he gathered his family, followers, and guards. He told them they were leaving Thebes. Some historians think he wanted to leave because he was afraid. Others think he finally decided to leave the city where he had spent so many unhappy years as a child. Whatever the reason, he took his new religion and the people who loved him and left Thebes to start a new life.

Chapter 4

Akhenaton led his family and followers through the desert, looking for a place to build a new city. He believed Aton would show him where to build. They traveled about 180 miles north of Thebes. Akhenaton then saw the sun rise on the horizon and rest in a gap in a mountain.

Akhenaton saw this as a sign from Aton. He decided to build his city on this spot in the desert. He called his city Akhetatet, which means "Horizon of the Aton." Today, the city of Akhetatet is known as Amarna (uh-MAHR-nuh), which is the name that will be used in this book to talk about Akhenaton's new city.

Amarna was on the east bank of the Nile River north of Thebes. It occupied a narrow strip of desert. It was 7 miles long, 3 miles wide, and surrounded by rock cliffs. This flat, sandy place was shaped like a crescent moon.

The first thing Akhenaton did was to have fourteen boundary markers, called *stella*, carved into the stone cliffs

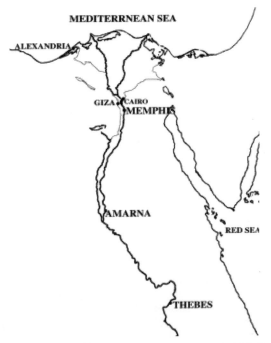

This map shows the location of Amarna, north of Thebes.

around his city. A priest in the 1700s discovered these three-thousand-year-old carvings. On the stella, there are hieroglyphs (HIE-ruh-gliffs), or pictures and symbols that made up the ancient Egyptian language. The hieroglyphs on the stella describe Nefertiti's beauty and Akhenaton's vision.

Akhenaton was the first Pharaoh to plan the layout of a city. Older cities in Egypt were built a little at a time, without a plan. Amarna was built in a hurry, but it was well thought out.

The buildings of Amarna were made with a new kind of mud brick that was smaller than the large stones used in other Egyptian cities. These small bricks helped speed up the building process. The small bricks were given a limestone covering and then covered with paintings and drawings. The bricks did not age well. Many of the drawings on them are chipped or worn away. This makes it difficult for archeologists to learn more about Akhenaton's life.

Historians do know that the city had a wide road going north and south along the Nile River. Akhenaton and Nefertiti used to drive down this road in their chariot. Sometimes they held chariot races on the wide road.

A covered bridge above the road connected the palace to the temple. A wide window called "The Window of Appearances" was built into the middle of the bridge. Akhenaton and Nefertiti looked down on the crowd from the window. Sometimes they would toss bread and gold necklaces down to the people who pleased them. Akhenaton wanted everyone to like him.

The palace was built around an open courtyard. In this courtyard was a zoo-like garden full of tropical plants and wild desert animals. The animals were gifts from neighboring countries. The palace kitchen was located outside and downwind, so the smoke would not blow back into the house.

The houses surrounding the palace were made of a sun-dried brick called adobe (uh-DOE-bee). Adobe is the same material that the Native Americans used for their houses in the southwestern United States. The houses in Amarna had baths and toilets that emptied out into the streets, which made huge garbage piles. Pigs roamed the streets, eating the garbage.

Ponds, fish tanks, and fountains were built in many places in the city. Many homes had a throne room and a chapel for praying to the Pharaoh and Aton. On the ground floor of the homes were cattle stalls. A stairway led up to the flat roof, which was used to store food.

Egyptologists believe 70,000 people lived in Amarna. Many of the people farmed the small piece of fertile ground near the Nile. They grew wheat, onions, and beans. Bread and beans were often served with fish or duck. The farmers were responsible for growing food for everyone. Some of the food was piled on the altar of the temple as an offering to Aton. The rest of the food was stored in the palace.

Akhenaton held court outdoors under the burning desert sun. He loved the sun. Because the sun was his god, it is not hard to imagine that he spent as much time in the sunlight as possible. Foreigners who visited Amarna complained about the heat and getting sunburned.

Akhenaton's city did not last long. The priests and people of Thebes destroyed the beautiful city of Amarna when Akhenaton died. For thirty-three centuries, the city lay buried beneath the desert sands. The lost city was found in 1845. With its discovery, archeologists began to realize there was even more mystery about Akhenaton.

Chapter 5

Another part of Egyptian life that Akhenaton changed was its art. Before his rule, Egyptian art had been the same for thousands of years.

All the sculptures of Pharaohs were designed the same way. They looked stiff and formal. In drawings, they looked young and muscular, seated on thrones or shown in battle. Their heads were always shown turned to one side.

Akhenaton gave his artists the freedom to draw or sculpt however they wanted. His motto was "living in truth." Stiff-looking art was replaced with a more realistic art form. Bodies looked rounder and more lifelike.

The artists drew his long head,

fingers, toes, and strangely shaped body. This idea of truth in art is also seen in later statues of Nefertiti, which show her with an old-looking body. Previous Pharaohs would never have allowed that.

Artists had the freedom to show the Pharaoh and his family as they really lived. Instead of battle scenes, artists showed scenes of family life in the royal palace. Akhenaton is shown with his wife sitting on his lap and their daughters climbing on them. Other drawings show Akhenaton as a family man, kissing and holding his daughters. This was a big change, because earlier art only showed the royal family in formal poses.

The foreigners who visited Akhenaton's court may also have influenced some of the changes in art. Akhenaton had special parties for the royal family, his high court, and guests from other countries. There are

This stella, Aton gives life to Akhenaton and his family as they enjoy each other's company.

drawings of acrobats and musicians. Groups of smiling guests are shown gathered around the performers.

Tomb drawings from Akhenaton's time period broke all the rules. They expressed emotion and showed movement. Papyrus (puh-PIE-russ) reeds seem to sway gracefully in the drawings. The use of chariots also gives the pictures a sense of movement. Chariots were drawn more often during this art period than in any other.

Some archeologists said that Akhenaton's art made the royal family look strange and ugly. Then, in 1912, a German archeologist found a statue head of Nefertiti. Archeologists began to think the Amarna artwork was beautiful. The German man could not describe how beautiful the statue was!

Akhenaton, who was left out of family pictures as a child, now had his

own artwork. He had convinced his artists to create new forms, but would he be able to convince the priests to accept his new religion?

©Photograph courtesy of the Rosicrucian Museum, San Jose, CA

Made in the 1920s, this is one of three direct replicas, or copies, of the Nefertiti Bust.

Chapter 6

For centuries, Pharaohs worshipped many gods, but Akhenaton believed in only one god. One way to understand Akhenaton is to look at how his religion affected him and Egypt.

When Akhenaton moved to Amarna, many priests stayed in the old capital, Thebes. Akhenaton thought these priests prayed to false gods. He ordered Egyptians to stop worshipping their many gods. Akhenaton also ordered his soldiers to destroy the false gods, erase their names from temple walls, and close the temples built for them. Many people secretly continued to worship the old gods.

Akhenaton ordered the people of

Egypt to take part in his new religion. This caused a great revolution. The mayor of Thebes was caught in the argument. By studying the mayor's tomb, historians think he was unsure about the changes Akhenaton made.

Two of the walls in the mayor's tomb were done in the traditional style. The other walls were painted in the artistic style that Akhenaton liked. On the walls built after Akhenaton's order, the mayor has a long face and wears a gold collar that Akhenaton may have given him so he would follow the new religion. When the mayor died, he may have been stuck between the old and new religions.

Archeologists also found many traditional gods in the homes of Akhenaton's followers in Amarna. Even they did not want to give up their old beliefs.

Ancient Egyptians were frightened by Akhenaton's interference with the afterlife. They believed the old gods helped them get into the next world. When people died, their internal organs were placed inside four separate jars (called canopic jars) in the tomb with four gods to protect them.

Akhenaton did not like anything the light of Aton did not touch, including the darkness of the afterlife and its old gods. He did not like the god Amun-Ra (AH-muhn-rah), because its name meant "Hidden One."

Many powerful priests in Thebes were very angry because the rebel

©Photograph courtesy of the Rosicrucian Museum, San Jose, CA

Canopic jars held the organs of the dead in ancient Egypt.

Pharaoh declared their gods dead. The priests probably wondered what would happen to themselves if there were no more gifts to the temples.

The priests used to take the prisoners of wars between Egypt and other countries as slaves or servants. Because Akhenaton didn't lead Egypt into any wars while he was Pharaoh, the priests did not get any new slaves.

Akhenaton tried to convince the priests to bring their requests to him so that he could pray to Aton for them. The rules of his religion said that only Akhenaton and Nefertiti could pray to Aton. This probably made the priests angry, because they now had even less power.

Akhenaton's religion remains a mystery because very little was written about it. The only record of his beliefs is a hundred-line song he wrote on the tomb walls, called "The Great Hymn to Aton." The song shows his devotion to an inner light. He said his god could not be compared to any other god. Akhenaton called Aton the creator of the universe and the father of all people.

Some historians think Akhenaton believed Aton was a god for people of distant lands, too. Records show that soldiers from foreign countries ate and drank together like brothers in Amarna. Akhenaton believed that the light of Aton shone on all people, making them all equals. Egypt was not a superior country, and they did not need to have an army to conquer other people. The world no longer revolved around Egypt. It revolved around the sun.

Not only did Akhenaton start a new religion, but it was the first to believe in only one god. Some historians think that Akhenaton's ideas influenced the ancient Jews. The Jews also believed in only one god and wrote down their beliefs in the Bible.

Chapter 7

Akhenaton's strange appearance is one of the biggest mysteries about this rebel Pharaoh. The statues and drawings of him show a weak and girlish-looking man. He had a huge, long head on top of a long, skinny neck. His chest was fleshy, and his stomach was round like a ball. His hips were wide, and his legs were long and skinny.

The first drawings of Akhenaton were almost cartoonlike. They showed a man who looked like a space alien. Egyptologists still do not know why his body was drawn this way. Perhaps Akhenaton's artists were experimenting with their new artistic freedom.

Nefertiti was also drawn like a cartoon with a long skull.

Akhenaton's appearance makes us ask many questions. Did he have an unknown disease? Or, as some people think, did he have the disease known as Marfan's syndrome? People with Marfan's are usually tall with a long, thin neck and chin. They usually have skinny arms and legs with long fingers and toes. Weak eyes and poor eyesight are also common with this disease.

People with Marfan's syndrome are usually sensitive to the cold. This may have been the reason Akhenaton liked the sun so much.

Pictures of Akhenaton's daughters also suggest that he may have had Marfan's syndrome. The disease is passed on to children. The princesses are all drawn with long skulls like their father. A statue of the head of Tutankhamen (too-tahng-KAH-muhn), or King Tut, also has this long shape.

We do not know if Akhenaton's artists made his children look like him to honor him, or if the children really inherited his appearance. When King Tut's skull was found, it showed his head as being a bit longer than most. The mystery continues.

This sandstone bust is of a daughter of Akhenaton. Notice the long forehead and skull.

Chapter 8

Akhenaton ruled Egypt from his desert city of Amarna for about ten years. Did he really rule Egypt, or did he stop caring about what was happening in his country?

There are no pictures of Akhenaton leading troops into battle, as previous Pharaohs did. There are only pictures of Akhenaton worshipping the sun disk. The lack of drawings of Akhenaton as a commander in battle makes Egyptologists think that he was more of a religious man. Akhenaton probably didn't want to be bothered with problems in neighboring lands. He left them to fight their own battles against invaders.

In the late 1800s, a local village woman found 350 clay tablets in Amarna. They have wedge-shaped marks on them called cuneiform (kyoo-NEE-uh-form) characters. These tablets became known as the Amarna letters.

The Amarna letters are part of Akhenaton's official notes. They were written to and from foreign kings about business dealings. When Egyptologists read the letters, they thought that Akhenaton didn't care about the business of running his country.

Other kings wrote to Akhenaton and asked for his help. Experts think Akhenaton ignored their needs, because they continued to find more letters. One letter asked Akhenaton to send troops before it was too late. Historians believe the writer needed help to fight off an invading army.

While Akhenaton ruled, Egypt's

once-great army became weak. Other countries stopped sending gifts to the Pharaoh. The huge empire that Amenhotep III left his son got smaller.

The longest-lasting mystery about Akhenaton began in the seventeenth year of his rule: He died and disappeared from all the historical records of Egypt.

How did Akhenaton die? Experts have many guesses. Some believe the priests of Thebes murdered Akhenaton because he closed their temples and started a new religion. Others believe that the military leader Horemheb (HOR-em-heb) ordered Akhenaton killed. General Horemheb was angry that the land he had fought for was lost during Akhenaton's rule.

After Akhenaton's death, no one was allowed to mention his name. The Egyptians buried their king, but when his tomb was found, it was empty. Some Egyptologists think the rulers who came after Akhenaton wanted to erase all memory of him, so they destroyed his mummy.

Still others think tomb robbers took it. The chief builders of the tombs and the high priests sometimes robbed the graves of Pharaohs because they knew the secret entrances. When a Pharaoh took the wealth of the country for himself, the priests did not get their usual gifts. They stole gold from the tombs to buy food for their families.

Akhenaton's mummy has not been found. His city of Amarna was left empty. He had given his followers gold and bread every day. Without Akhenaton to feed them, his followers returned to Thebes. Akhenaton's religion also died. The sun disk, Aton, was replaced with the old gods. Amarna existed for only twenty-five years, and then it disappeared beneath the blowing desert sands. It would not be discovered for thousands of years.

Chapter 9

Akhenaton was gone. He had been erased from memory. His city was emptied and destroyed. Yet more mysteries remain to be solved. Was Akhenaton the father of King Tut? Many people believe he was, although there is no real evidence to prove this.

The early drawings of the royal family show Akhenaton, his wife Nefertiti, and their six daughters. In later pictures, when Akhenaton was in the last years of his rule, there is little mention of Nefertiti. Did she fall out of favor with the Pharaoh because she didn't give birth to a son? Did she die? No one knows.

Most archeologists think Akhenaton

had another wife named Kiya (KEE-yah), who was King Tut's mother. There are drawings of Kiya on the tomb walls. Unlike Queen Nefertiti, Kiya is never shown wearing a crown or helping with religious ceremonies. Kiya never appears in the same picture with Nefertiti. Writing on the tomb walls says that Kiya was the great beloved wife of the king, but Nefertiti was the great royal wife.

Kiya is shown with a daughter but not a son. However, even if King Tut were Akhenaton's son, he would not have appeared on the tomb walls. Sons were not usually shown on tomb walls because the Pharaohs thought that would weaken their own power.

In 1922, archeologist Howard Carter found King Tut's tomb in the Valley of the Kings. He searched for five years before he found it. Never before had a tomb been found with all of its treasure untouched.

King Tut's gold death mask was one of the many treasures found in his tomb.

Some scholars believe King Tut lived in Amarna but soon moved back to Thebes. There are some drawings of King Tut swimming in the Nile with the royal family, but Akhenaton is not in any of these pictures. There are also pictures of King Tut in his chariot hunting for ostriches.

Some Egyptologists believe that they found Akhenaton's mummy in the Valley of Kings. Scientific testing can prove if he was father to both King Tut and Smenkhkare (smeng-KAR-eh), another Pharaoh. Until Akhenaton's mummy is positively identified, this part of the mystery cannot be solved.

Chapter 10

The first few years after the death of Akhenaton are also filled with mystery. We do not know who became the next Pharaoh. There are many guesses, but no definite proof. There are those who believe Smenkhkare, the eldest son of Akhenaton and Kiya, became the ruler. Others believe the ruler was the young King Tut.

Archeologists and Egyptologists found a mystery mummy in a tomb they named KV 55. At first, Egyptologists thought the long-lost mummy was Akhenaton. When they looked closer, they agreed that the mummy was too young to be Akhenaton.

This mummy was buried in a body-shaped coffin called a sarcophagus (sar-COFF-uh-gus). Even though many historians believe that the mummy is the body of Smenkhkare, no one can prove this.

Egyptologists have tried to create a time line that shows what might have happened after Akhenaton's death. They think that Smenkhkare ruled first for a very short time. When he died, Tut became the next male in line to be Pharaoh.

His half-sister Ankhes (AHNK-ehs) became his wife and queen. Perhaps Aye (rhymes with *pie*), the high priest, told Tut and his sister Ankhes that they had to leave Amarna and return to Thebes, where Akhenaton built his first temple. When Tut left Amarna, he was very young. It took one week to travel the 150 miles to Thebes by boat. This must have been quite an adventure for a young boy who had never been outside his father's desert city.

Tut was crowned Pharaoh in the city of Thebes. He was only nine years old. The double crown of Upper and Lower Egypt was placed upon his head. He was given a crook and flail to hold. These were the symbols of royalty.

At first, High Priest Aye and General Horemheb probably ruled for King Tut because he was so young. It was also possible that it was General Horemheb who gave the order to have the city of Amarna and the temple of Aton destroyed.

After Tut became Pharaoh, he made a law called the "Restoration Stella Act." With this act, King Tut promised religious freedom and the rebuilding of the old temples. He made this law to make the priests who had lost everything during Akhenaton's rule happy again. Making this law was probably the high priest's or the general's idea.

From the drawings found in King Tut's tomb, Egyptologists think that King Tut and his wife, Ankhes, liked each other as they became teenagers. There is a picture of King Tut hunting for fish and birds in the marshes with Ankhes by his side, handing him arrows for his bow. Another drawing shows the sun disk, Aton, shining down on the two of them as she gave him flowers. This is the only drawing of Aton. Later drawings show the couple with the sun god, Ra.

Two small coffins were found in King Tut's tomb. Egyptologists think that Ankhes was pregnant with a daughter, but the baby died in the eighth month, before it was born. This happened to Ankhes twice and was not the last tragedy of her life.

After ruling fewer than ten years, King Tut died. Because Tut's tomb had never been disturbed, Egyptologists were able to gather evidence about his death. At first, there were two different opinions. Some believed he was murdered, but others thought he died of an illness. Tut was just eighteen years old when he died.

In 1978, an X-ray was taken of Tut's skull. It showed that he had been hit on the back of his head. Experts can only guess who hit him and whether or not it caused his death. In many ways, King Tut's death also remains a mystery.

Chapter 11

When King Tut died, Queen Ankhes was the last person in the royal family. As the daughter of Akhenaton, Ankhes knew the man she married would become the next Pharaoh. Ankhes wrote to the king of the Hittites, an enemy of Egypt. She asked the king to send his son to marry her and become Pharaoh of Egypt. She was looking for someone to protect and support her.

The Hittite king did not believe Ankhes. She sent a second letter, begging the king to send a son for her to marry. Finally, the enemy king agreed.

Time was running out. Ankhes had to marry quickly. She had only seventy days while King Tut's body was being made into a mummy. After that, a new Pharaoh would be crowned.

The young Hittite prince never arrived. He was killed on his way to Egypt. Who killed the prince? Was it Aye, the high priest? Was it General Horemheb, who hated the Hittites and fought them in several battles? No one knows.

Some of the historians believe Ankhes married Aye, who might also have been her grandfather. He was about sixty years old at the time and had been the high priest for many years. Aye was also one of the men who made decisions for the young King Tut. Others think that if Aye was Pharaoh, it was only for about three years.

Ankhes died a few years after King Tut. Her death is also a mystery, because her mummy and tomb have not been found.

After Aye and Ankhes died, the next person to get power to rule was General Horemheb. To understand some of the mysteries, it is important to know the part General Horemheb played in the lives of Akhenaton, King Tut, and Ankhes. General Horemheb tried to erase Akhenaton from Egyptian history.

At a temple to Amun-Ra, there is proof. General Horemheb wanted to get rid of all the "rot" that Akhenaton and his sons left behind. As the Pharaoh, Horemheb was determined to make Egypt powerful again.

For sixty years, he tried to change what he thought Akhenaton did

©Mesopotamian Museum of Art, Gift of Mr. and Mrs. V. Everit Macy, 1923. Photograph ©1979

This statue of Horemheb was made when King Tut was Pharaoh.

wrong, first while he was a general, then for twenty-seven years when he was Pharaoh. Horemheb put the old gods back into the Egyptian religion, got rid of people in the central government that did not agree with him, and made the army stronger.

In 1978, a French archeologist found 20,000 small stone blocks stacked inside the walls of Horemheb's temple. They were carved with hieroglyphs.

The blocks were called *talatat*, which is Arabic for "three hands," because they were as long as three hands. The archeologist realized that these blocks were from Akhenaton's tomb. Even though many of the blocks were worn or damaged, some still had pictures painted on them.

An American Egyptologist took pictures of the blocks and then scanned them into a computer to try to match them. As more of the blocks were found, the number grew to 100,000.

About half of the blocks had pictures on them.

The American realized the blocks were from four different temples. Almost 2,000 matches have been made with these blocks. They show what life was like in Amarna. They are still being pieced together today.

Another expert began to wonder why the blocks were hidden in Horemheb's temple. One archeologist believed Horemheb hated Akhenaton so much, he took Akhenaton's temple apart block by block. Horemheb hid the blocks in his own temple in Luxor, then declared that he had been Pharaoh since the day Amenhotep III died. This wiped out Akhenaton's entire rule.

Horemheb tried to destroy everything Akhenaton created, but he did not succeed. However, he did add to the mysteries about Akhenaton's life.

Chapter 12

Ancient Egyptians believed a Pharaoh could live forever in the afterlife if people remembered him and did not destroy his mummy. By pretending that Akhenaton never existed, Horemheb did the worst possible thing to him. The Egyptians called it a double-death––to die and then to be forgotten.

Ancient Egyptians left good records of the past. Their preparations for the afterlife preserved their way of life on tomb walls for future generations. However, in the case of Akhenaton, more than three thousand years passed before his city was found. Much remains unknown about this strange

Pharaoh.

Some archeologists believe that Akhenaton was the first person to start a new religion that believed in only one god.

Was Akhenaton a failure as a Pharaoh? He didn't seem to care about the business of running a kingdom. He was more interested in peace than keeping his country strong. Some Egyptologists consider him a tragic figure because his changes did not last. His city was destroyed and his religion was lost.

Ideas are not as easy to destroy as people and cities. The art of Amarna continued to influence the next generation of artists. Figures in drawings and sculptures became more relaxed. The drawings of the royal family's daily lives seemed to send a message of love, as did Akhenaton's "Hymn to Aton." Like the art, the writing style became less formal and took a poetic turn.

General Horemheb and the priests erased Akhenaton's name from the list of Egypt's kings. Even so, he is not forgotten. More than two thousand books have been written about him and the Amarna period of Egyptian history.

If Akhenaton's mummy is ever identified, many of the mysteries surrounding his life may be solved. Until then, Akhenaton's legend and mystery live on.

Bibliography

Aldred, Cyril. *Akhenaton: King of Egypt.* New York: Thames and Hudson, 1988.

Brier, Bob. *The Murder of Tutankhamen: A True Story.* New York: Putnam, 1988.

Edwards, I. E. S. *The Treasures of Tutankhamun.* New York: Penguin Books, 1976.

Gore, Rick. "Pharaohs of the Sun." *National Geographic.* April 2001. 34-57.

Hayes, Michael. *The Egyptians.* New York: Rizzoli, 1998.

Hornung, Erik. *Akhenaten and the Religion of Light.* Ithaca: Cornell University Press, 1999.

Papanek, John L. *Lost Civilizations: Egypt, Land of the Pharaohs.* Alexandria, Va.: Time-Life Books, 1992.

Redford, Donald B. *Akhenaten: The Heretic King.* Princeton: Princeton University Press, 1984.

Russman, Edna. *Ancient Egypt: Discovering its Splendors.* Washington, D.C.: National Geographic Society, 1978.

Artesian Press

High Interest...Easy Reading

Other Nonfiction Read-Along

Disasters

- Challenger
- The Kuwaiti Oil Fires
- The Last Flight of 007
- The Mount St. Helens Volcano
- The Nuclear Disaster at Chernobyl

Disaster Display Set (5 each of 5 titles 25 books in all)
80106

Natural Disasters

- Blizzards
- Earthquakes
- Hurricanes and Floods
- Tornadoes
- Wildfires

Disaster Display Set (5 each of 5 titles 25 books in all)
80032

www.artesianpress.com